SACRED

SATB and organ

OXFORD

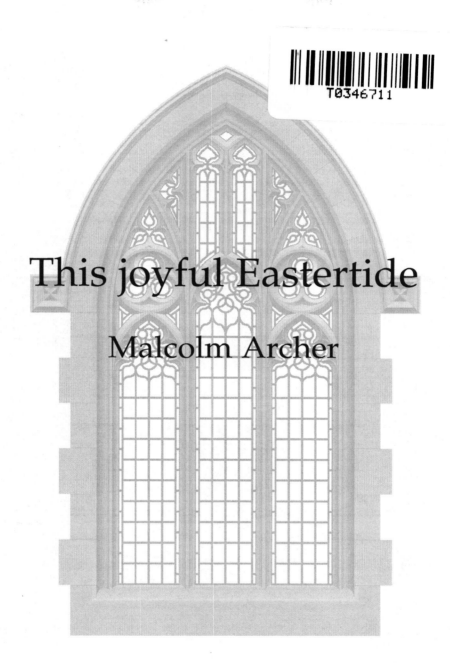

This joyful Eastertide

Malcolm Archer

MUSIC DEPARTMENT

OXFORD
UNIVERSITY PRESS

for Daniel Hyde and the choir of King's College, Cambridge

This joyful Eastertide

G. R. Woodward (1848–1934)

17th-cent. Dutch
arr. MALCOLM ARCHER

Duration: 3 mins

Printed in Great Britain

OXFORD UNIVERSITY PRESS, MUSIC DEPARTMENT, GREAT CLARENDON STREET, OXFORD OX2 6DP

TENOR & BASSES *unis.* **mf**

My Love, the Cru-ci-fied, Hath sprung to life this

S. **mp**

A.

Had Christ, that once was slain, Ne'er burst his

T.

mor - - - row.

B. **mp**

three-day pri - son,_____ Our faith had been in vain:_____ But

Ch. 8', 2'

mp

X835   This joyful Eastertide   ARCHER

ISBN 978-0-19-356029-1